The Everyday Guide to Primary Geography: Story

Julia Tanner and Jane Whittle
Series Editor: Julia Tanner

Series introduction

Geography is a vitally important component in a rich, broad and balanced primary curriculum. It is a subject which is driven by curiosity about the world as it is now and how it might change in the future. It provides the knowledge, understanding and skills necessary to address the great social, economic, environmental and ethical challenges which face humankind in the 21st century. It involves not only finding out where places are and what they are like, but also investigating how they have evolved and changed in the past, and how they may develop in the future. It enables children to make sense of places they know from first-hand experience, and of the wider world they have yet to explore. It helps them to understand their place in the world, and how people and places are linked at every level from local to global. It invites them to consider the impact of their actions on the environment, what they value locally and globally, and how they can contribute to the creation of a better future.

As series editor, I hope to inspire you to engage in active 'curriculum making' by providing stimulating ideas which you can adapt, extend or modify to meet the needs and interest of your class and your school's curriculum. All the activities are tried and tested, demonstrating how everyday and easily accessible resources, used creatively, can enhance and enrich pupils' geographical learning. Each double page is divided into panels with the key geographical learning opportunities on the left, supported by downloadable resources available from the webpage for this Guide (see below).

High-quality geographical work incorporates three key interrelated elements (Table 1). The first of these is an enquiry approach that involves asking geographical questions and using a range of skills, some specifically geographical, to find the answers. The second is the study of places, such as the local area, town, region, country or, at a global scale, continent, or the whole world. The third element involves learning about the physical and/or human and/or environmental geography of the places studied. Combining these different elements can enable pupils to think geographically in authentic learning activities which have real purposes, audiences and outcomes.

Enquiry, geographical skills and fieldwork	Asking and answering questions Planning and undertaking geographical enquiries Communicating the outcome of enquiries Making and using maps Fieldwork skills Using secondary resources such as books, websites, images Understanding differing points of view
Studying places – place and location knowledge	The school grounds and local area The UK, Europe and the wider world Localities in the UK, Europe and the wider world Locational knowledge
Physical, human and environmental geography	**Physical geography** • landscapes, volcanoes, rivers, coasts • the weather, seasons and climate • landscapes, plants and animals **Human geography** • homes, buildings, villages, towns and cities • journeys and the movement of people, goods and ideas • jobs, agriculture, fishing, mining, manufacturing, transport, services • land use and the location of activities **Environmental geography** • change and development • caring for the environment and the planet • sustainability and environmental responsibility

Table 1: The three elements of high-quality geographical work

This series illustrates the amazing scope of geography in the primary curriculum, and the stimulating range of learning approaches it encompasses. It showcases high-quality geographical work contributed by primary classes in the UK and beyond. I hope it will be an inspiration to you to create challenging, exciting and satisfying geographical learning experiences for the pupils you teach.

Julia Tanner, July 2013

Resources to accompany this Guide, such as activity sheets, teacher guidance, extra activities and cross-curricular links, are available to download from the Geographical Association website.
Go to **www.geography.org.uk/everydayguides**
Click on the button for this Guide and then enter the password **TW83XY**

Contents

Geography through story 4

Eliza and the Moonchild by Emma Chichester Clark 6
Investigating the school grounds

The Shepherd Boy by Kim Lewis 8
Life on a sheep farm in northern England

Oliver Who Travelled Far and Wide by Mara Bergman and Nick Maland 10
Fantasy introducing rainforest, desert and high mountain environments

A Balloon for Grandad by Nigel Gray 12
A balloon flies from the UK to an island in the Nile

We all went on Safari by Laurie Krebs and Julia Cairns 14
Counting story set in the East African plains

Voices in the Park by Anthony Browne 16
A walk in a local urban park

Eco-Wolf and the Three Pigs by Laurence Anholt and Arthur Robins 18
Retelling of the classic story with an environmental twist

Mirror by Jeannie Baker 20
Parallel stories of everyday life in Australia and Morocco

Hey! What's that Nasty Whiff? by Julia Jarman and Garry Parsons 22
Environmental story set in the African savannah

Mia's Story by Michael Foreman 24
A story of life and change set in Chile

Flotsam by David Wiesner 26
An ancient camera travels the oceans

Belonging by Jeannie Baker 28
Picture book illustrating the greening of an urban neighbourhood

The Other Side of Truth by Beverley Naidoo 30
Two Nigerian children find themselves refugees in London

In the Bush: Our holiday at Wombat Flat by Roland Harvey 32
A camping trip in the Australian outback

Kensuke's Kingdom by Michael Morpurgo 34
A round the world sailing trip ends in shipwreck on a tropical island

Useful resources and websites 36

Geography through story

This Guide is about the use of high-quality picture, story and fiction books to stimulate, enliven and enrich geography at key stages 1 and 2. It demonstrates a wide range of practical classroom strategies for using fiction to develop pupils' geographical thinking, knowledge and understanding, and extend their geographical skills. It also explores some rich possibilities for cross-curricular work through linking geography with literacy and other subjects.

The aims of the Guide are to:
- demonstrate the value of story as a vehicle for promoting geographical thinking, including geographical vocabulary and positional and locational language
- exemplify strategies for developing geographical skills, such as enquiry, map work, fieldwork, visual literacy, making comparisons, etc., through picture, story and fiction books
- illustrate creative ideas for enhancing pupils' knowledge and understanding of places, and of physical, human and environmental geography through story
- provide valuable ideas and resources to use in the classroom.

The value of story

Stories are a universal aspect of human societies and cultures around the world. Whether oral or written, they are capable of capturing our hearts, minds and imaginations. As Cremin states 'it is widely recognised that narrative pervades human experience; in dreams and daydreams, anecdotes, jokes and arguments, it is a way of thinking about the world and shaping experience within it' (2009, p. 101). Sharing high-quality books in the classroom brings places, characters and events to life. Many teachers routinely make excellent use of story as part of their teaching repertoire, recognising its potential and power for enhancing learning across the curriculum.

As noted in the series introduction, high-quality geographical work incorporates three interrelated elements – enquiry and skills; places; and physical, human and environmental geography. Story books provide endless opportunities to explore all three aspects of geography.

The advantages of using picture, story and fiction books in geography teaching and learning are manifold.

- Well-chosen books have a powerful impact in the classroom; they can engage pupils' interest, excite curiosity, provoke questions, pose dilemmas and spark imaginative responses.
- Stories are engaging and accessible for all pupils, including those with limited literacy skills, and provide excellent stimuli for a wide range of thought-provoking learning activities and cross-curricular work.
- All stories are set in a real or imagined location and many books convey, through text and illustrations, a strong sense of place. Exposure to books with an evocative sense of place will extend pupils' knowledge and understanding of different types of locations and the people who live, work and play in them.
- Stories set in familiar environments such as schools, towns or parks help pupils make connections between their own experiences and their emerging knowledge and understanding of these places.
- Many stories are set in locations beyond pupils' own experience, so expand their horizons, transporting them to new, unfamiliar, and sometimes unimagined, places and environments.
- The themes in children's literature often explore important aspects of physical, human or environmental geography, such as the weather, journeys or the impact of development.
- Strong plot lines often involve moral, social and environmental dilemmas, which engage pupils' emotions as well as minds. Such storylines encourage exploration of different viewpoints and generates informed debate of the issues raised.

Why use story in geography?

Geography as a subject in the primary curriculum is concerned with people and places and the interaction between the two. It focuses on the interconnectedness of people, places and environment and encourages pupils to enquire into these connections at every scale from local to global. Geography has a vital role to play in helping pupils understand the world in which they are growing up, and in equipping them with the knowledge, understanding and skills to be active, informed and responsible citizens.

- Evocative illustrations can provoke awe and wonder at the beauty of the landscapes, plants and animals of the natural world, as well as at the amazing buildings, structures and other achievements of humankind.
- As works of fiction, stories are open to alternative understandings and endings, encouraging imaginative responses. Books with relevant themes inspire creative thinking about real-life environmental and social justice challenges.

Using this Guide

This Guide has been written for classroom teachers, trainee teachers and teaching assistants working in primary schools. It will also be a useful resource and reference work for geography co-ordinators or subject leaders, and senior leaders responsible for whole-curriculum planning or the quality of teaching and learning. The Guide will be of interest to educators who are excited by holistic and creative approaches, and to those who believe that primary pupils learn best when they are stimulated and motivated by engaging and challenging learning activities.

The aim of this Guide is to encourage the use of story and picture books in primary geography teaching and learning. To support this aim, the Geographical Association (GA) has compiled an extensive database of over 200 children's books, organised by age range and relevant geographical themes (see right for details).

This Guide features 15 high-quality children's books. Each double-page spread provides brief information about the picture or story book itself, outlines several ideas for using the book with pupils, and gives information about relevant additional resources to extend the work. The potential of each book for geographical learning is detailed on the left-hand page, where opportunities for developing geographical enquiry and skills, and key knowledge and understanding are also listed. The ideas for learning activities illustrate some of the possibilities each book offers for motivating and challenging geographical learning activities, and are often accompanied by examples of pupils' work. There are also links to additional resources on the web page for this Guide (see right).

The 15 featured books reflect the diverse range of high-quality children's literature available. They have been chosen to illustrate the huge potential for developing geography through story across the primary age range. Although the books are presented in approximate age range order – from key stage 1 through lower key stage 2 to upper key stage 2 – several could be used with a wide age range. The teaching ideas are flexible – most can be adapted for younger or older pupils, or for those with differentiated learning needs. Many of the specific suggestions for learning activities can be applied to other books.

We hope this Guide will reveal the exciting potential for geographical work through the stimulus of story, and encourage teachers to experiment with the suggestions offered. Books can stimulate pupils' interest in and curiosity about the world, and open their hearts and minds to new possibilities and ways of thinking. They are an essential resource for a rich, meaningful and satisfying geographical education.

Web-based resources

Each double-page spread has additional web-based resources. These include:
- key vocabulary
- cross-curricular links
- web links and resources
- activity sheets
- examples of pupils' work
- instructions
- additional activities

As an additional resource, this Guide has an accompanying children's books spreadsheet, organised by key stage, and geographical places and themes:
- geographical enquiry
- use of maps and atlases
- map making
- use of secondary sources
- scale
- local area
- UK localities/places
- non-UK localities/places
- wider world
- weather/seasons/climate
- biosphere/biodiversity
- landscapes/mountains/rivers
- settlements
- economic/leisure activities
- transport/travel/journeys
- environmental change/issues
- global citizenship
- sustainable development
- fantasy

Go to www.geography.org.uk/everydayguides to download the resources.

Reference

Cremin, T. (2009) *Teaching English Creatively*. Abingdon: Routledge.

Eliza and the Moonchild
Emma Chichester Clark, Andersen Press (2008)

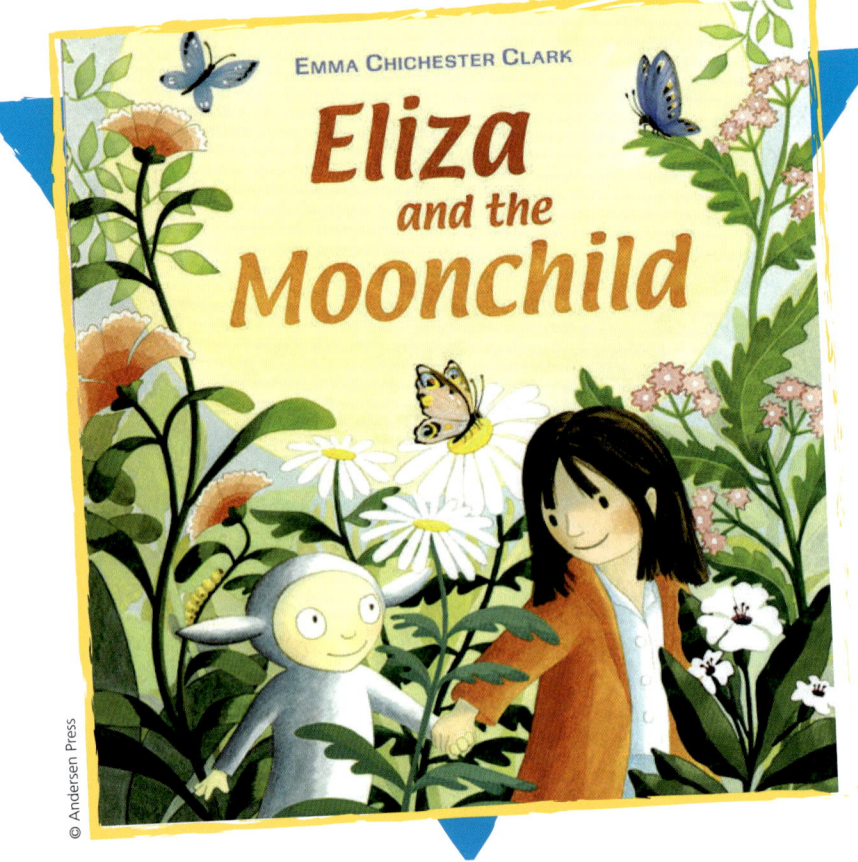

This book is set on the moon and in a roof-top garden in an urban environment

Geographical enquiry and skills

- visual literacy
- enquiry skills – asking and answering questions
- using geographical vocabulary
- fieldwork – observing, identifying and recording
- map work – finding locations and planning routes

Geographical knowledge and understanding

- features of the school grounds
- features of gardens
- what makes places attractive
- the concept of scale
- the concept of near and far

Reference

Tanner, J. (2009) 'Special places: place attachment and children's happiness', *Primary Geographer*, 68, pp. 5-8.

To access extra resources from the Everyday Guides web page, see page 2.

Moonchild is a boy who lives on the moon. While everything on the moon is monochrome, Moonchild dreams of a world filled with colour. After seeing planet Earth through his telescope, Moonchild travels there in his Moon-Zoom machine and meets Eliza. Moonchild is initially disappointed with Earth because he cannot see any of the colours he dreamt about. As the sun rises, however, a world of colour comes to life. Eliza paints a picture of all the beautiful things Moonchild has seen for him to keep as a memory. Back on the moon, Moonchild creates his own paintings. The twist in the story is revealed in the final image: Eliza has shown Moonchild her roof-top garden, a colourful oasis in a grey urban environment.

Sharing the book

While reading *Eliza and the Moonchild*, ask pupils to pay particular attention to the colours used in the images. What sort of a place is it? What do these colours tell them about the place? Where could it be? What season could it be? Why are there so many/few colours?

At the end of the story, when the illustration zooms out, it reveals that the story setting is in fact Eliza's roof-top garden in an urbanised area. Revealing this will spark lively discussions and questions. It is an opportunity to ask: Are you surprised by where Eliza lives? Why does Eliza have a garden like this? What else can you see in Eliza's local area?

Teaching activities

Colour catching

This is a simple fieldwork activity in the school grounds. Explain that the pupils can find many different colours outside, and that they are going to 'catch' some colours just like Eliza and Moonchild do in the book.

At this point, one of the following activities could be undertaken:

- Give pupils a colour mat and ask them to find objects that match the different colours. This will promote an investigative approach and encourage pupils to study the school grounds. Encourage them to look high and low, under objects, around corners, etc., investigating the natural and built environment.
- Prior to the lesson collect empty egg boxes and paint each egg pocket a different colour. Ask pupils to search for items of these colours. They could then sort the objects into natural and man-made items.
- Divide the class into small groups and provide each group with a camera. Groups take photos of interesting objects of different colours. Once the photographs are printed, ask pupils to sort them according to colour or other criteria.

As an extension, pupils use a simple map of the school grounds to plot where the objects were found, or the photographs taken. You could make an interactive display, inviting pupils to match the objects or photographs to their correct location on the map.

Taking Moonchild around the school grounds

Pupils make their own cardboard cut-out figure or puppet of Moonchild (or another young alien creature), whom they show around their local area, just as Eliza does in the story. Discuss what Moonchild might find interesting in the school grounds. Pupils could draw or write about what they would like to show Moonchild. They then plan a route, and record this on a map of the school grounds.

Carry out the walk, asking pupils to talk to their cut-out figure or puppet about the things they see. Take photographs and record some of the oral contributions to create a multimedia display.

Encourage creative play in the role play area and provide materials for pupils to sit and paint – just as Moonchild and Eliza do in the story. They may like to create pictures of the school buildings and grounds. Display the paintings with pupils' annotations, or make them into a book entitled 'Special Places in Our School Grounds'. For more ideas for encouraging children to notice and appreciate their school grounds and local area see Tanner (2009).

Making model gardens/moonscapes

Re-read the text, focusing on the features of the garden. Ask questions to encourage close observation and extend pupils' thinking: What can you see? What is this? Why is it there? How does it grow? Is it natural?

Explain to the class that they are going to recreate Eliza's garden and/or Moonchild's home. Ask them to think about how they could make or paint the features and where to put them. Provide resources for them to create model gardens and/or moonscapes. Encourage imaginative play with the cut-out Moonchildren or other miniature figures.

Modelling real or imaginary places provides lots of opportunities for using vocabulary to name and describe geographical features. If both Moonchild's and Eliza's worlds are modelled, there is the opportunity to compare the two environments.

Improvement project

The colourful beauty of the plants and flowers in Eliza's garden is a key theme of *Eliza and the Moonchild*. Is there is an area of your school grounds that would be improved by adding some planters, creating a new flower bed or some other initiative? Involve pupils in planning and working on this improvement project.

The Shepherd Boy

Kim Lewis, Walker Books (1991)

This book is set in rural Northumberland, England

Geographical enquiry and skills

- enquiry – asking and answering questions
- using and understanding geographical vocabulary
- visual literacy – using pictures to find out about places
- making comparisons between places

Geographical knowledge and understanding

- life and work on a sheep farm
- seasonal change and activities

To access extra resources from the Everyday Guides web page, see page 2.

© Sheffield Tiger (Creative Commons licence)

This is the story of 5 year-old James who longs to be a shepherd like his father. As he is too young to join in, James has to watch his father tend the sheep through the changing seasons, using his toy lamb to act out the farming activities – lambing, shearing, dipping and feeding. At Christmas, James is overjoyed to be given a sheepdog puppy and, come the spring, he and his dog join his father in tending the sheep while his toy lamb lies neglected at home...

In addition to the geographical themes of life on a sheep farm and seasonal change, this book also explores significant emotional issues, including the relationship between father and son and outgrowing beloved toys. Much of the story is told through evocative illustrations of life on the farm.

Sharing the book

Show pupils the cover but hide the title. What do they think the book might be about? What sort of place is shown on the front cover? What can they see? Reveal the title, and ask pupils what they think a shepherd does. Record these ideas for future reference. Read the story, discussing the pictures. What have pupils learnt about what shepherds do? Might there be some other tasks not shown in the book? Add any new tasks to their original list.

Teaching activities

Living on a sheep farm

Pupils imagine themselves on a sheep farm (they can draw themselves on a sticky note, and place it on one of the pictures in the book). What can they see, hear, smell in this place? How do they feel? Ask if they would they like to live on a sheep farm, and discuss their reasons with a talk buddy. Separate the class into two groups: those who would and those who wouldn't like to live on a sheep farm. Record the reasons for their choices, creating a list of ideas about the good and bad things about living on a sheep farm. Does anybody want to change their mind having heard all the opinions? Pupils could record this activity pictorially and/or by writing about why they would/would not like to live on a sheep farm.

The seasons

Pupils look for clues about different types of weather and seasons in the book, and consider what seasonal changes they see in their own environment (weather, trees, clothes people wear, etc.). Draw their attention to the seasonal nature of tasks on a sheep farm. Why do they think this happens in spring/summer/autumn/winter? Do they or their families do different activities in different seasons? You could create a chart/diagram showing typical seasonal activities on a sheep farm. Alternatively, pupils can create books showing a year in their lives, illustrating what they do as the seasons change, e.g. play seasonal games. This could be developed as an imaginative task in which pupils think about what they would like to do in the next year. These activities would enrich topic work on the weather or seasons.

Rural or urban?

This idea will work best in schools in urban environments. Pupils think about how their local area compares to the rural environment depicted in *The Shepherd Boy*. To support thinking about differences, ask what they can see in the pictures that they would not find in their local area, what is in their local area but not in the book and what is common to each place. Pupils are likely to find it easier to think of differences rather than similarities, so challenge them to find things in the book that are the same (e.g. changes in the weather and seasonal change, people live in houses in both places). Record the similarities and differences. Read other books by Kim Lewis set on a sheep farm (see the Everyday Guides web page for link), and find out more about living in a farming community.

Following this discussion, introduce the terms urban and rural. Encourage pupils to search through their class library to look for examples of illustrations set in urban and rural areas. Create an interactive display of images and key vocabulary associated with rural and urban places. Provide opportunities for pupils to match and sort images and words to develop their understanding of the characteristics of rural and urban places.

Role play

Encourage imaginative social play by turning the role play area into somewhere shown in the book, such as the farmhouse kitchen or the barn, or perhaps an associated rural place such as a vet's surgery or the office at the sheep auction. Pupils will need to consider the features of the place, the people likely to be there, and the situations that might arise. Involve pupils in setting up these areas, discussing what they would expect to find in such places. How might a rural vet's surgery be different from an urban one? What notices or information would be on the wall of a sheep auction office? What might the phone calls to a shepherd be about?

Visiting a farm

Pupils always enjoy a visit to a farm; it enriches their knowledge and understanding of farms and farmers' role in producing food and managing the countryside. Advice and guidance on organising farm visits is available from Farming and Countryside Education. The Federation of City Farms and Community Gardens website has a very useful education section and interactive map for locating a farm in your area (see the Everyday Guides web page for links).

Oliver Who Travelled Far and Wide

Mara Bergman and Nick Maland, Hodder Children's Books (2009)

This book portrays rainforest, desert and mountain environments

Geographical enquiry and skills

- enquiry – asking and answering questions
- using and understanding geographical vocabulary
- visual literacy – using pictures to learn about different types of environments
- using globes and atlases

Geographical knowledge and understanding

- different types of environments
- the relationship between weather/climate and physical environment
- different sorts of journeys

To access extra resources from the Everyday Guides web page, see page 2.

Oliver Who Travelled Far and Wide describes the adventures Oliver has when he wakes up during the night and discovers that his teddy bear is missing. Accompanied by Bat, Owl and Fox, Oliver travels on his toy train through many different environments until Ted is finally rescued from a bird's nest high on a snowy mountain. The short text includes lots of rhymes accompanied by bold stylised illustrations.

Sharing the story

Start by looking closely at the front cover and discussing the title. What might this book be about? While you read the story aloud, pupils might like to join in with Oliver's actions (Oliver asleep, waking up, looking under the bed, peering through the binoculars, etc.). The book also lends itself to prediction, using both the words and the pictures as clues to what might happen next.

Ask pupils if they have ever lost a treasured toy and what they did to find it. This discussion will provide plenty of opportunities to use locational language such as under, in, behind, between, outside. The activity 'Where's Teddy?' (page 11) also provides opportunities to practice using locational language.

Teaching activities

A letter from Ted

How did Ted get into the bird's nest? Reading a letter from Ted, asking for the pupils' help to solve this mystery will encourage careful scrutiny of the pictures, some of which reveal helpful clues. This could also be the stimulus for creative work, with pupils' creating their own version of the story told from Ted's point of view. They could make picture books, a frieze or picture maps to show Ted's journey from the bedroom to the tree. An example letter can be found on the Everyday Guides web page.

Where's Teddy?

Pupils take it in turns to hide a toy when no one else is looking. They can then give directions to help others find the toy, perhaps offering additional information as the seekers get closer (e.g. 'He is near the sink', 'He is underneath something red'). Older or more able pupils could write their instructions as if they were the toy (e.g. 'I am near the classroom door, underneath something soft and green'). These activities will encourage the use of locational vocabulary.

Unfamiliar environments

Oliver Who Travelled Far and Wide illustrates several different environments: a tropical rainforest, an arid desert and snow-covered mountain peaks. Pupils should study the pictures carefully; although the illustrations are rather stylised, they include many accurate geographical features. Ask them:

- What sort of place is this? Introduce relevant vocabulary – tropical rainforest, desert, forest, mountains.

- What can you see there? Introduce the vocabulary to name and describe the features, plants and animals. For example, the tropical rainforest picture shows lush vegetation including trees, ferns, flowers, monkeys and birds.

- What do you think the weather is like in this environment? Help pupils to understand the connection between the weather, climate and type of environment.

- Have you ever been to a place like this? Discuss what they remember and what it felt like to be there. If pupils have photographs of themselves in any of these environments, ask them to bring copies into school.

Use an environmental globe or atlas map to find the places in the world where tropical rainforests, deserts and mountainous regions are located. Ask pupils to find pictures of these sorts of environments and display them adjacent to a world map. If they bring in photographs of themselves in relevant environments, display the images with strings showing the locations where they were taken.

Imaginative play

Use imaginative play with small world models such as a train set and puppets/other toys to recreate the story. Alternatively, pupils can invent their own versions of the journey taken by Oliver and his toys, or imagine and create other journeys using different forms of transport, such as boats, cars or aeroplanes.

A Balloon for Grandad
Nigel Gray, Orchard Books (2002)

The story starts in suburban England and shows a balloon's journey across the Alps, the Mediterranean Sea and the Sahara Desert to Northern Sudan

Geographical enquiry and skills

- enquiry – asking and answering questions
- visual literacy
- atlas and map reading
- route finding and recording
- compass work
- comparing places
- discussing emotional responses to places

Geographical knowledge and understanding

- long-distant journeys
- major geographical features (the Alps, Sahara Desert, etc.)
- contrasting landscapes
- settlements in different places
- scale (of the different places represented)
- non-UK localities

To access extra resources from the Everyday Guides web page, see page 2.

Sam keeps his red balloon with silver stars by the back door. When it is carried away by the wind, Sam is extremely upset, and Dad comforts him. Together, they imagine that the balloon is going to visit Sam's Grandad Abdulla. They think about the amazing journey the balloon will have and how happy Grandad Abdulla will be to see his gift from Sam. This delightful picture book portrays the journey of the balloon across Europe to Northern Sudan and will spark curiosity about distant localities.

Sharing the book

As you share the book with pupils, discuss the story. Re-read the text, stopping for pupils to look carefully at each of the illustrations. Ask pupils which is their favourite place in the story and to explain why. Provide sticky notes showing emoticons (happy faces, worried faces, sad faces, etc.), and ask pupils to choose one to represent how they would feel in each place. Listen to pupils' reasoning and encourage discussion.

Use atlases and globes to locate the places shown in the book then mark the route taken by the balloon on a large world map. Discuss the distances, e.g. is Sudan near to or far from their school?

Using the page where Sam's Dad describes the balloon's route and the thinking routine 'odd one out', encourage pupils to find similarities and differences between the pictures. For example, they may notice houses in two of the pictures and not in others. Challenge them to find as many examples as possible, looking carefully at all elements of the pictures. Guidance on using the 'Odd One Out' thinking strategy can be found on the web page for this Guide (see page 2).

Once pupils are familiar with searching the pictures, turn to the double-page spreads of places the balloon travels over and ask them to name what they see, e.g. mountains, church, cows, bird, in the Alps picture. Record each word on a separate sticky note, using different colours for each location – perhaps green for the mountains, blue for the sea and yellow for the desert. Invite pupils to sort the sticky notes into different categories.

Teaching activities

Our balloon's journey

A Balloon for Grandad depends on the idea that the wind blows the balloon south-east from England to Northern Sudan. Prepare a balloon with a label asking whoever finds it to post the label back to the class saying where it was found. Release the balloon outside the school. Watch it take flight, noticing the direction it travels. Watch the balloon for as long as possible and ask pupils to think about what is beneath it as it travels. Provide maps and atlases for pupils to identify the probable route of the balloon, and discuss the features and places it will pass. When the label is returned, locate the place it was found on a map or in an atlas and compare this with the pupils' predictions.

Wind direction and speed

Every day, observe the wind direction and speed. This provides a meaningful context to make weather observations, use a compass and directional language, and keep records. A simplified form of the Beaufort scale will help pupils develop the vocabulary associated with wind speed.

When the wind is blowing in a different direction from the day you released your balloon, hand out long strips of paper and ask pupils to imagine the route a balloon would take that day, given observed wind direction and speed. They will need access to maps and atlases to predict and draw the route. They should share their ideas and explain reasons for their predictions. Where would a balloon go? Would it land in the local area or travel further afield?

Where do our grandparents live?

Ask pupils to think about where their grandparents and other family members and friends live, involving parents if necessary. Do they have a grandparent or other family member/friend who lives at some distance? Ask them to send a postcard of the place where they live to the class. As the postcards arrive share each one with the pupils, and use maps and atlases to find the places. Discuss the route a balloon would take if it blew from school to that place. Create a display of the postcards alongside a British Isles or world map, as appropriate.

Pupils could make picture books in the style of *A Balloon for Grandad*, using pictures to show the journey a balloon would take to reach a chosen family member/friend.

Interactive display

Create a display about *A Balloon for Grandad* using some of the following ideas.

- A list of the different locations that the balloon flies over. Pupils should sequence these in the correct order. Where does the balloon fly over first, next, last?

- Pictures of the localities the balloon flies over drawn using Microsoft Paint (or other similar program). Pupils should replicate the important features, including the balloon. Print the pictures and encourage pupils to sort these in different ways.

- A frieze of the different localities the balloon passes over. Place a card balloon threaded on string above the images so pupils can re-tell the story, moving the balloon along the route.

- Recording postcards. Thinking about their emoticon stickers (see left), pupils explain how they might feel at various points along the balloon's route. Their responses are recorded and attached in the appropriate place. Pupils should listen to others' opinions and discuss whether they agree or disagree.

- Key vocabulary in balloon shapes. Pupils can then use these words when interacting with the display.

- Print images of different localities sourced from the internet and provide pupils with a cardboard balloon: ask them to place their cardboard balloon above the photographs and describe the landscape using directional or locational language.

We all went on safari
Laurie Krebs and Julia Cairns, Barefoot Books (2003)

This book is set in the Serengeti, Tanzania

Geographical enquiry and skills

- enquiry – asking and answering questions
- using and understanding geographical vocabulary
- visual literacy – using pictures to learn about the landscape of the Serengeti
- using globes and atlases

Geographical knowledge and understanding

- the location of significant places related to the book (UK, Africa, Indian Ocean, Tanzania, etc.)
- the landscape, climate and animals of the Serengeti
- the Maasai people

Reference

Leeds DEC (1996) *Feeling Good about Faraway Friends*. Leeds: Leeds DEC.

To access extra resources from the Everyday Guides web page, see page 2.

© Koen Muurling (Creative Commons licence)

This beautifully-illustrated picture book follows a Maasai family as they travel through the Serengeti grasslands in East Africa. As the sun rises the family encounters one leopard, then two ostriches, three giraffes, etc. until, late in the afternoon, they encounter ten elephants. The book contains facts about Tanzania and a simple map of the country, as well as information about the Maasai people, their lifestyle, and the animals the family meets. The book also offers opportunities to learn a few words in Swahili.

Sharing the story

Start by looking at the illustration on the front cover and discussing the title. What can pupils see? What is a safari? Read the book. Pupils will soon join in with the simple rhyming text. Some of the animals mentioned will be familiar from picture books, television and films, while others, such as wildebeests and warthogs, may not. Use the pictures to encourage pupils to describe these animals. Pupils will probably enjoy hearing the story more than once, becoming more familiar with it on each re-reading.

Teaching activities

Imagining the Serengeti

Movement activities will help pupils engage more deeply with the story. Working in a room with sufficient space, pupils imagine that they are in the Serengeti and experiment with moving like the different animals in the story. Use appropriate language and voice tone to help them represent the ways the different animals move – the slow lumbering elephant, the swift-moving long-legged ostrich and the hippopotamus wallowing in the lake. Pupils could also act out the journey of the Maasai family as they traverse the Serengeti, miming their reactions to the different animals, e.g. caution near the leopard and lions, pleasure in the antics of the monkeys. Enhance the activities by playing Tanzanian music in the background.

Finding out about the Serengeti and Maasai

The evocative illustrations in *We All Went on Safari* convey a sense of the space and beauty of the Serengeti (meaning 'endless plain' in Swahili). On a second or third reading, use the pictures to draw pupils' attention to the landscape. What is the Serengeti like? What sort of clues can they see? They should name and describe the landscape features (e.g. the grasslands, the mountains beyond), and the variety of trees and plants. From the pictures, what do they think the weather is like in the Serengeti? Pupils may suggest that it is hot and dry but you can challenge this common misconception by asking how the grass and trees could grow if there is no rain. Remind them that plants need water to grow.

Show pupils the map at the back of the book, then find Tanzania on a globe or in an atlas. Look first for the pupils' own country, then Africa, the Indian Ocean, Lake Victoria, and finally the Serengeti National Park. This structured focusing process will help pupils relate the location of the story to their place in the world, and build their locational knowledge of the wider world.

Some pupils might like to find other features shown on the map, such as Mount Kilimanjaro, the Great Rift Valley, Arusha, Dar es Salaam and the neighbouring countries of Kenya, Zambia and Mozambique. Use a globe or world map to discuss how they could get to the Serengeti, thinking about both the route and modes of transport.

The resource pack, *Feeling Good about Faraway Friends* (Leeds DEC, 1996), provides excellent resources and activities for pupils to learn about the Maasai people and their lifestyles.

Modelling the Serengeti

Pupils could create models of the Serengeti landscape in cardboard boxes. Allocate small groups different animals which feature in the story, and ask them to research each animal's habitat using books, images and other information. The finished models can be exhibited like display cases in a natural history museum, complete with supporting information boards.

Alternatively, pupils may enjoy recreating the setting for the story using miniature animal and people figures in the sand tray or on the floor. The play will be enhanced if you are able to provide relevant landscape features (grass matting, trees, etc.) and some adult support to exploit the rich language development opportunities this sort of play offers.

A local counting book/frieze

Use *We All Went on Safari* as a stimulus to create a counting book or frieze set in your local area. When pupils go for a walk in the local area, what animals and birds do they see? Replicating the format of the book will encourage pupils to think about wildlife in their local area, and offers plenty of opportunities for cross-curricular work.

Voices in the Park
Anthony Browne, Corgi Children's Books (1999)

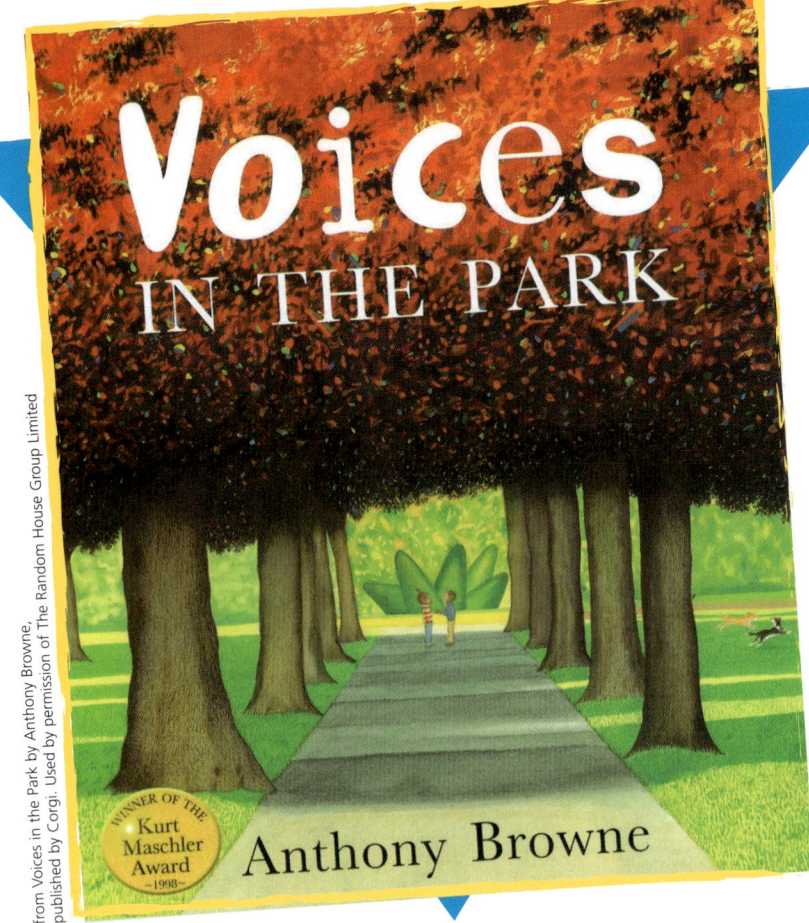

This book is set in an imaginary and surreal urban park

Geographical enquiry and skills

- visual literacy
- enquiry – asking and answering questions
- planning, conducting and reporting an investigation
- recording field data
- map work – recording field data and proposed improvements
- empathy – appreciating differing points of view
- creating a presentation

Geographical knowledge and understanding

- the importance of parks for a local community
- leisure activities in parks
- people want different things from shared (public) places
- potential conflict in shared (public) places

To access extra resources from the Everyday Guides web page, see page 2.

Voices in the Park tells the story of a visit to the park. It is divided into four parts, each telling one character's version of events. The illustrations and well-crafted text show that these events happened simultaneously. The book explores the range of activities that happen in a park, however, the illustrations provide twists in the plot. It focuses on journeys, activities and the emotional attachments people make to a park and to one another. Therefore, the book is a powerful cross-curricular resource, demanding more than one reading – and each picture invites close scrutiny.

Sharing the story

Encourage pupils to think about how authors create a sense of place with words and pictures by reading the story very slowly. As you do so, ask pupils to draw what they think the park looks like from just the language used in the story and the image on the front cover. When the reading is complete, ask pupils to share their drawings and then reveal the book's images in order to make comparisons. Were their perceptions of the park correct? Ask what would have helped them to make more accurate drawings. Pupils may find drawing the park difficult as the text has minimal description – Anthony Browne relies instead on the images to convey the sense of place. As a shared writing activity, look at each illustration and write captions using geographical vocabulary to name and describe the park's features. Look at other picture books and discuss the role of illustrations and text in establishing a sense of place.

Teaching activities

Our voices in the park

Invite pupils to think about their own experience of parks. Where is their favourite park? What is their favourite memory of it? Ask them to remember this as they draw and annotate a picture of it. Collate and display the work, or make a book entitled 'Our voices in the park'. If pupils have photos of themselves at their favourite park these could be displayed alongside a map.

Local enquiry and fieldwork

A key theme of *Voices in the Park* is the different experiences the characters have during their visit to the park. Discuss who visits your local park – mention children, dog walkers, joggers, older people, parents with babies/toddlers, tennis or bowls players, Local Authority gardeners, teenagers, ice cream van owners – and what these different people want from it.

Explain to pupils that they are going to undertake an enquiry on their local park and how it could be improved, they will then make recommendations to local councillors. Many councillors will be pleased to attend school to meet pupils and discuss their ideas. Where this is not possible create and send a written report or digital presentation to the Council.

As a class, use a KWHL grid to plan the enquiry. Record what they already know (K), what they want to know (W) and how they plan to find out (H). At the end of the investigation, record what they have learnt (L) (see KWHL chart on the Everyday Guides web page).

Taking digital cameras, maps of the park and notepaper, visit the park. Investigate the facilities it has, then discuss and record how attractive it is to visit. Pupils should keep the enquiry idea in their minds at all times.

After walking around the park, bring the class together and ask them to think about a specific aspect of the park. For example: What do they like/dislike about the park? Who was there? What were they doing? What facilities are there for different park users? How could it be improved to better meet their needs? How accessible is the park?

Back at school, allocate each group a different sort of park user to consider. Use KWHL grids to plan group enquiries. Invite pupils to record what they have found out, and what more they would like to know before making suggestions for improvements. This may include interviews with park users, questionnaires to the local community and further visits to the park, as well as research on other parks. Ask each group to make a map and a report/presentation to show and justify the improvements they would like to see to make the park better. Conclude with the groups presenting their case to a local councillor.

Remind pupils that their voices/opinions are very important, and consider what practical action they could take to make a difference to the park.

An alternative perspective

The dogs, Victoria and Albert, feature on most pages of the book. Re-read the text looking at the dogs' movements and use the illustrations to form a more detailed understanding of Victoria and Albert's part in the story. Divide the class into pairs to make maps of the park. When the maps are complete, the pairs take on the roles of Victoria and Albert. Encourage pupils to think about the text and work together to draw the route the dogs take in the story. They could also write the fifth and sixth version of the story – the story from Victoria's and Albert's perspectives (see example on the Everyday Guides web page). Pupils should use their map and the book to help them create a story rooted in the story's sense of place – the park.

Colour, Symbol, Image (CSI)

Ask pupils to think about what they saw in *Voices in the Park* and their feelings towards it then complete the colour, symbol, image (CSI) chart (available to download from the Everyday Guides web page). First, pupils should choose a colour that they think most represents the images in the book; this will be challenging as there are many contrasts of colours throughout the book. Next, ask them to draw a symbol that represents the ideas of the book. Finally pupils draw an image that represents the place, feelings and concepts of the book. Following each section, pupils write a justification for their thinking.

Eco-Wolf and the Three Pigs

Laurence Anholt and Arthur Robins, Orchard Books (2002)

This book is set in an imagined beautiful valley, Eco-Wolf's local area

Geographical enquiry and skills

- geographical enquiry – asking and answering questions
- using geographical vocabulary
- planning an enquiry into the sustainability of the local area of the school
- investigating the sustainability of the school grounds and the locality

Geographical knowledge and understanding

- the local area – Eco-Wolf's valley
- issues of sustainability in a local area
- the impact of development in a local place
- different attitudes to the same place
- different views on development of a valley

To access extra resources from the Everyday Guides web page, see page 2.

Eco-Wolf lives in a beautiful valley where he respects nature and lives sustainably. Eco-Wolf has a happy life until one day three big bad pigs arrive to build houses in the valley. They set to work immediately, cutting down precious oak trees to build luxury homes. With the help of the other animals (and some huffing and puffing), Eco-Wolf manages to destroy the new homes. This does not deter the pigs who make several more attempts to build houses. Following the pigs' third attempt, Eco-Wolf convinces them to help clean up the valley and make it a sustainable place. The three pigs learn vital lessons about polluting and destroying a precious place.

Sharing the story

Pupils will enjoy hearing this story a number of times and taking on the different voices of Eco-Wolf and the three pigs. Explore the idea that the Valley is Eco-Wolf's local area. Encourage pupils to think about what happens to his place as a result of the pigs' actions, and the impact on Eco-Wolf, the environment and the other animals who live nearby.

Create an art gallery: mount photocopies of each illustration in the centre of a large piece of paper and display them around the classroom. Pupils move around the gallery looking at the illustrations, when they hear a shaker or similar musical instrument (played by you) they stop next to the nearest picture. Explain that each of the illustrations portrays a message about what is happening in Eco-Wolf's local area. Ask pupils to record what they think is happening by writing on the paper around the image. This activity can be repeated several times, giving pupils the opportunity to read their peers' ideas and either agree or challenge them in their discussions.

Teaching activities

Positive minus interesting

To record pupils' ideas about the book in a creative way, as a class construct a PMI (Positive, Minus and Interesting) chart (available to download from the Everyday Guides web page). This strategy encourages focused and analytical thinking.

- What positive things happen to Eco-Wolf's local area in the story? Why is it a positive place to live? What positive actions does Eco-Wolf take in his local area?
- What negative (minus) things happen to Eco-Wolf's local area in the story? What negative actions happen in the story?
- What do pupils find interesting in the story? Encourage them to think about new vocabulary, ideas or character relationships.

Local area enquiry

Plan and undertake an enquiry into sustainable development in your local area. You could focus on a generic question (such as 'Do we live sustainably in our local area?'), investigate a specific local development proposal (such as a plan to build a new road or housing estate), or devise proposals to improve opportunities for local residents to live in a more sustainable way. Your enquiry will be more successful if the pupils are involved in choosing the topic, planning the investigation and working collectively towards presenting the outcomes to a real audience.

Different groups could investigate different aspects of the enquiry question. This allows pupils in each group to become 'relative experts', acting as reference points for other members of the class. Each group should use a KWHL chart to plan their investigation (available to download from the Everyday Guides web page).

The groups should think about the materials as well as what steps they will need to take to complete their enquiry. Each group should decide how best to present their findings to the rest of the class – through a presentation, poster, bulletin board, model, play, interactive display or website.

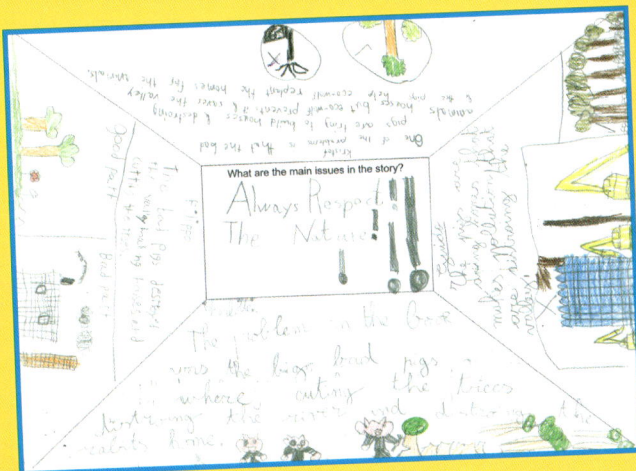

Bottoms up!

Divide the class into groups of four. Give each group an A3 sheet with the key question 'What are the main issues in *Eco-Wolf and the Three Pigs*?' in a box in the centre. The rest of the page should be divided into four boxes so that each member of the group has a section to write and draw in.

In their groups, pupils respond individually to the key question, writing their thoughts in their respective boxes. The activity takes its name from the fact that all four pupils will have to kneel up – with their bottoms in the air – to all write on the paper simultaneously! Pupils share their answers with their group then summarise the group's thoughts in the central box. This will encourage discussion and ensure that pupils focus on the key information in the story to answer the central question. Pupils will naturally want to share and compare their summarised responses with the class and an effective extension question could be: 'How do these issues relate to our local area?'.

© Ruth Potts

Once the presentations have been completed, pupils may have many ideas of ways to communicate their findings more widely. Audiences could include the school council, local politicians, planners or a local community/residents group. Pupils could create a website, organise a campaign, or take personal action to live more sustainably.

At the end of the enquiry, ensure there is an opportunity for pupils to reflect on the whole process. Remind them of the main enquiry question and ask them to think about their findings. Encourage pupils to complete a thinking routine 'I used to think... but now I think...' on sticky notes or slips of paper to show that such an enquiry can lead to a change of thinking or a deeper understanding. Pupils may find they did not fully answer all the questions. Discuss this, developing the idea that not all enquiries lead to one definitive answer.

Mirror
Jeannie Baker, Walker Books (2010)

This book is set in suburban Sydney, Australia, and the Valley of the Roses, Morocco

Geographical enquiry and skills

- enquiry – asking and answering questions
- visual literacy
- comparing places – finding similarities and differences
- fieldwork – observation and recording of local buildings

Geographical knowledge and understanding

- everyday life in Sydney (Australia) and the Valley of the Roses (Morocco)
- physical geography – natural landscapes, weather and climate
- human geography – buildings, built landscapes, land use; different forms of travel and transport; economic activity (jobs, retail parks and markets)
- connections between places

To access extra resources from the Everyday Guides web page, see page 2.

Mirror is a book of two stories and two cultures. Using collage and fabric art, it depicts life in Sydney, Australia, and the Valley of the Roses, Morocco. The two stories are designed to be read simultaneously, from the left and the right. The title and explanation for the book are written in English and Arabic. As you open the book you are presented with quadruple page spreads which show early morning in the two places. The wordless story follows two boys and their families through a morning, concluding with after lunch images illustrating the connections between the two places. The fabulous collages reveal many details of landscape and life in the two locations, and the structure of the book naturally provokes discussion of similarities and differences.

Sharing the book

Take time to look at the front and back cover to elicit pupils' ideas about what *Mirror* might be about. Opening the book will raise questions about its design and format. Before reading the book, ensure pupils understand that *Mirror* should be read in terms of two parallel stories running together. Spend some time on each page, asking pupils to comment on what they see in both the foreground and background.

Teaching activities

Comparing localities

Following a shared reading, use a globe or atlas to find Sydney and the Valley of the Roses and discuss their location. How could we describe where they are found? (northern/southern hemisphere, continent, country). When pupils are familiar with the locations, re-read the story, ensuring the corresponding pages are turned simultaneously. This will stimulate a discussion of the similarities and differences between the Valley of the Roses and suburban Sydney. The discussion could focus on a different element during each re-reading (e.g. landscape, homes, journeys or economic activities). Record pupil observations on a comparison chart, systematically looking for evidence of physical and human geographical features such as the landscape, weather, buildings, landuse, jobs, leisure activities and everyday life (clothing, food, etc.). A recording sheet is available to download from the Everyday Guides web page.

Collage landscapes/townscapes

The collage illustrations in *Mirror* evoke a strong sense of place, and pupils will be fascinated by the textures and detail. This book acts as excellent inspiration for creating collages of landscapes or townscapes. A walk in the school grounds or the immediate locality of the school should provide plenty of stimulus. Encourage pupils to make sketches and take photographs to use in the classroom. Investigate how Jeannie Baker creates her collages on her website (see Everyday Guides web page for link) and ask pupils to experiment with different collage materials and techniques. Creating individual or group collages will provide a meaningful context for the use of geographical language, and provoke in-depth consideration of how places can be represented through visual media.

Replicating the book

Re-read *Mirror*, asking pupils to think about the time of day represented in each picture. What can they tell about the time of day from the pictures? The story unfolds in six time periods: getting up; breakfast; after breakfast; before lunch; lunch; and after lunch.

Ask pupils to think about one day of their weekend. What happened in each of the six time periods? Where did they go? What did they see? Using a 3 x 2 table ask them to storyboard the events following the same time framework as in *Mirror*. Ask them to think about and highlight the key events/places on their storyboards.

Invite pupils to make their own books to illustrate their weekend day, inspired by the format in *Mirror*. Show them how to adapt their storyboard into pictures, emphasising the importance of representing that place in their own pictures. Point out that we only know where *Mirror* is set because the natural and built landscapes are so accurately illustrated.

Once pupils are familiar with the idea of changing their storyboards into pictures, divide the class into pairs and give each pair two blank books to work on. Encourage the pairs to work together to ensure that the corresponding pages of each book represent the same time period. Remind them that one pupil will be working from the front of their book and the other from the back. Where appropriate, replicate the dual language aspect of *Mirror*, using languages known by the pupils or the modern foreign language studied. Once the books are completed, attach them to a front cover and ask pupils to work with their partner to think of a title and suitable illustration.

It may be useful to construct a prototype book to help pupils understand how the final versions will be assembled – see the Everyday Guides web page for more information on this.

Hey! What's That Nasty Whiff?

Julia Jarman and Garry Parsons, Scholastic (2010)

This book is set in the African savannah

Geographical enquiry and skills

- enquiry – asking and answering questions
- visual literacy
- locating places using globes and atlases
- using secondary resources to investigate places

Geographical knowledge and understanding

- ecosystem of the African plains
- biodiversity
- the 3Rs (reduce, reuse, recycle) and composting
- environmental issues – protecting the planet at local and global scales
- sustainable lifestyles

To access extra resources from the Everyday Guides web page, see page 2.

This rhyming book tells the story of Hyena who, with the help of Vulture, spends every day looking after her locality, the African savannah, by recycling, cleaning and tending her compost heap. When Hyena realises her hard work is going unappreciated, she and Vulture take a holiday. With Hyena and Vulture away it is not long before the rubbish mounts up and starts to stink! The other animals soon beg Vulture and Hyena to return. The story ends with all the animals promising to behave more responsibly and help to save the planet.

Sharing the book

As you read, allow pupils to enjoy the rhyming pattern and comical illustrations, then read it again, asking them to listen and look for the ways that Hyena and Vulture care for their local environment. There are lots of images of Hyena doing jobs to look after her local area. Study each one, asking pupils: How is Hyena helping the environment? How can people live like Hyena? Discuss why people recycle waste, compost and save water. As a class or in small groups, create a table to show the jobs Hyena does, the positive effects they have on the local area, and the negative effects that occur when Hyena stops doing the work.

To summarise pupils' ideas, create a conscience alley. Choose one pupil to play the part of Hyena and divide the class into two lines. One side gives reasons for Hyena to stay and continue her work, while the other tries to persuade Hyena to go on holiday (see above). When pupils have prepared their ideas, ask Hyena to walk down the alley listening to each pupil's reason for or against staying. At the end, the pupil playing Hyena explains their feelings and why they were persuaded by one side.

Extend this activity by asking pupils to think about why we need to protect the planet and discuss ideas as a group, perhaps through a circle time or a Philosophy for Children (P4C) session.

Teaching activities

Investigating the 3Rs

In the story, Hyena makes good use of natural resources by managing waste well. Introduce pupils to the 3Rs of waste management – reduce, reuse, recycle – and explore current methods of waste disposal and their impact on our environment. Encourage them to think about recycling in the news and some of the more controversial aspects of recycling.' Pupils could contact the Local Authority to find out what happens to waste from school and home, and investigate how it is disposed. Use the internet with pupils to investigate local opportunities for sustainable disposal of unwanted items, recycling rubbish and composting garden waste. If possible, organise a fieldtrip to a local recycling point or centre.

Our environmental contract

Turn to the page where Vulture says he is going to draw up a contract for the animals. There is lots of writing on the contract but it is not clear what it says. Encourage pupils to think about what they can do in school and at home to limit the amount of waste they produce. Ask pupils to consider what would be on an environmental contract for the school. Create one as a class, and share it with a real audience such as the school council or headteacher.

The Keep Britain Tidy website provides information about eco-school awards, and the Reduce, Reuse, Recycle site offers useful guidance on making your school more sustainable as well as relevant learning and teaching resources (see Everyday Guides web page for links).

Savannah ecosystems

Use an atlas to locate the African savannah, and grasslands in other continents. Can the pupils see a pattern in where these habitats are located? Create a map to show the global distribution of grasslands and their names (including the prairies in North America, pampas in South America, steppes in Asia and rangelands in Australia).

Ask pupils to use library books and the internet to investigate how savannah and other grassland ecosystems operate. They should find out about the weather, climate, landscape, plants and animals. Challenge pupils to produce a poster, flow chart or web diagram to show how these factors are interrelated in creating the ecosystem.

Many endangered species live in grassland environments. Encourage pupils to choose one endangered animal and investigate the threats to it; they can also look at what can be done to protect it. Many conservation charities provide excellent resources to support this activity.

An emotional symphony

Re-read the story stopping at the Pong and Poo page.
Ask pupils to look at the animals' reactions and to consider what each is thinking and feeling and why. Place a piece of A3 paper on each table (one for each animal), asking small groups of pupils to visit each animal and write down some ideas. Share the ideas then explain that pupils are going to represent the animals' emotions using sound – an emotional symphony.

Assign a small group to each animal. Give pupils time to think about the ideas and to attach sounds and words to how the animal is feeling.

Bring the class together. Acting as the conductor of a symphony orchestra, explain that when you point at a group they should begin their sound. Repeat until all the groups are making their sounds then point to individual groups again to signal they should fade their sound out to silence. Repeat the activity, asking pupils to reflect:
- What kind of sounds did you hear?
- What words describe the emotions shown in the sounds?
- Why did we hear these sounds?

To extend the activity, create an emotional symphony for the final page of *Hey! What's that Nasty Whiff?* to contrast the emotions of environmental change in the story.

Mia's Story
Michael Foreman, Walker Books (2006)

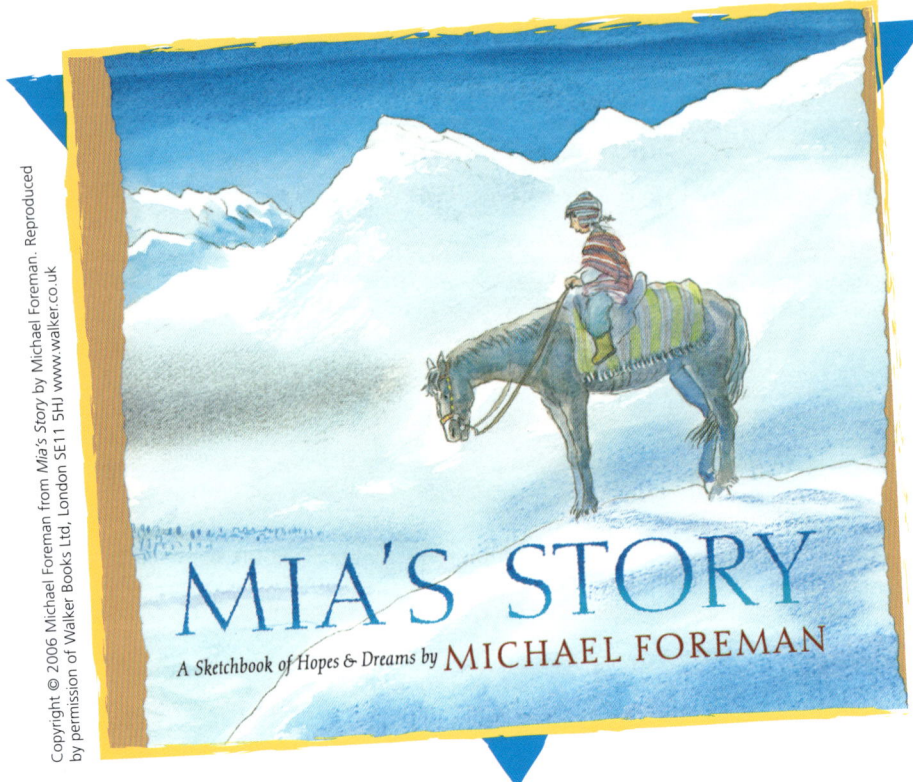

This book is set in Santiago and a village in the foothills of the Andes, Chile

Geographical enquiry and skills

- enquiry – asking and answering questions
- using and understanding geographical vocabulary
- atlas work – locating places, describing locations
- visual literacy – using pictures to find out about places
- making comparisons between places

Geographical knowledge and understanding

- the location of South America, Chile and Santiago
- daily life in Chile
- the characteristics of rural and urban places
- the possibilities for reusing and recycling 'rubbish'
- change in places

Reference

Tanner, J. (2012) 'How do you see it?', *Primary Geography*, 78, pp. 22–3.

To access extra resources from the Everyday Guides web page, see page 2.

Mia's Story was inspired by Michael Foreman's travels in Chile. After leaving Santiago, his bus broke down and he found himself in a village where the farmland had become a huge rubbish dump for the city. There Foreman met Manuel, Mia's father, who told him how the villagers scavenged on the rubbish site, finding, recycling and selling usable items. The book tells the story of how Mia goes high into the Andes looking for her lost dog. There, she finds some flowering plants, which she takes back to her village, where they quickly spread. Next year, the flowers cover the rubbish dump. Mia goes with her father to the city, where her plants prove very popular with customers in the city's cathedral square. Although a child, she has helped to transform her village and the fortunes of her family.

Sharing the book

Start by looking at the front cover with the pupils: What do they think the book might be about? What sort of place is shown on the front cover? What can they see in the picture? Read the story, looking carefully at the illustrations – many of which are in the style of an artist's sketchbook. The illustrations provide many details about life in Mia's village and the market by the cathedral in the centre of Santiago. Ask pupils to think about the places in the story – Mia's village, the mountains and Santiago city.

Teaching activities

Put yourself in the picture

This deceptively simple activity (adapted from Tanner, 2012) works particularly well with picture books that have strong visual images of place, such as *Mia's Story*. After reading the story and discussing the illustrations, ask pupils to draw a picture of themselves on a sticky note. They imagine themselves on a magic carpet being whisked to the story setting. To help them concentrate, ask them to shut their eyes and imagine the sensation of the movement through the air. Then allow them to place their sticky note in the book where they have 'landed'. What can they see, hear, smell? How do they feel, finding themselves in this place? This can be developed into imaginative role play, small world play, or a movement or drama activity. Alternatively, you might like to use this activity as a stimulus for exploring the affective impact of the pupils imagining themselves in different types of places.

Locating places

Use a globe and/or an atlas to find Chile, Santiago and the Andes. Challenge pupils to find different ways of describing the location of Santiago, such as 'It is south of the equator', 'It is a long way from here', 'It is near the Pacific Ocean'. Provide useful sentence starters such as: It is near to…; It is far from…; It is north/south/east/west of…; It is 100km from…; It is nowhere near…

Comparing village and city

This activity is very useful for helping pupils to compare places, identifying ways in which they are similar and different. It focuses on the questions 'What are these places like?' and 'How are they similar and different?' Ask pupils to look carefully at the village and city illustrations in *Mia's Story*, naming all the things they can see. Encourage them to describe the details of the landscapes shown, the buildings, the open spaces, the people and their activities. Draw a large Venn diagram, labelling the two outer sections 'village' and 'city' and the middle section 'both'. Pupils can record their observations by drawing and labelling the features they see in the correct segment of the Venn diagram. When they have finished, ask them why they think some features (such as houses) are found in both places, while others (such as the cathedral) are only in one.

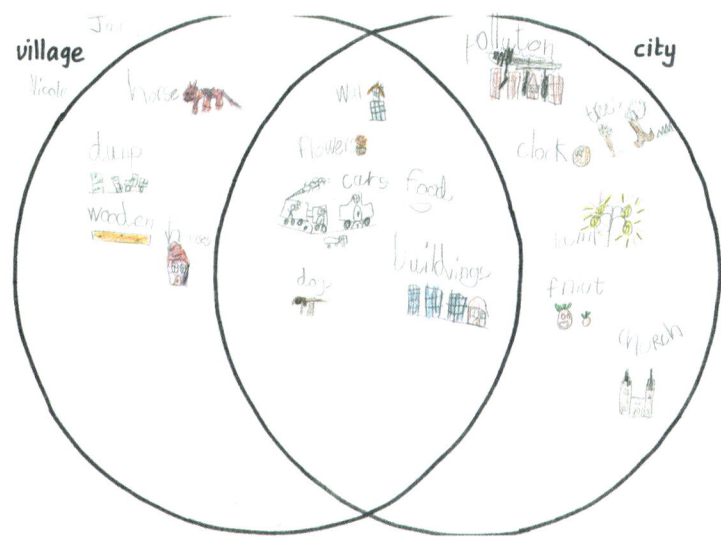

Changing places

A major theme of *Mia's Story* is the change that happens when the plants Mia brings down from the mountain naturalise and transform the village landscape. She then sells these in Santiago, contributing to the family income. Ask pupils to reflect on what the village is like before and after this happens. They can record their thoughts on the activity sheet 'Changing places', available from the Everyday Guides web page.

Flotsam
David Wiesner, Houghton Mifflin (2006)

© jdnx (Creative Commons licence)

This book is set on beaches, and in fantastical underwater environments

Geographical enquiry and skills

- enquiry – asking and answering questions
- visual literacy – interpreting photographs
- using geographical imagination
- making maps of imaginary places
- route planning
- locating, comparing and contrasting coastal localities

Geographical knowledge and understanding

- the concept of home – what does a home look/sound/feel like?
- ocean life
- tides and coastal processes
- travel and journeys

To access extra resources from the Everyday Guides web page, see page 2.

In *Flotsam* a boy is happily playing on a beach when an ancient camera is washed up on the shore. Taking the film to be developed, he is amazed at what he discovers: a series of surprising photographs of ocean worlds. There are homes, living things and much, much more... The last print depicts a girl, holding a photo of a boy, holding a photo, and so on. As the images become smaller, the boy views them through his magnifying glass and then his microscope. The sequence of photographs of children continues back through time, ending with a sepia image. After photographing himself holding the print, the boy throws the camera back into the sea, where it is carried away by the waves for another child to find.

Sharing the book

Flotsam presents a fantastical view of ocean life entirely through pictures and encourages reflection about the power of photographs to capture snapshots of time and place. When you first read the story, use questioning and discussion to ensure pupils understand the plot. Pupils will enjoy the detail in the illustrations, so allow plenty of time for them to study the pictures.

Teaching activities

Travelling camera

The photographs in *Flotsam* show that the camera has travelled widely, washing up on beaches throughout the world. Challenge pupils to guess where these beaches are, based on the information contained in the illustrations. If they threw a waterproof digital camera into the sea, where would they like it to end up? Can they plot a route to their chosen destination? What photographs would they take to show the finder what their home, school and local area is like? What photographs would they like the finder to take before casting the camera into the ocean again?

Behind the door

Ask pupils to choose a page/location that particularly interests them (e.g. the sea turtle's house, the mermaid world). They then make a list of the features they can see. Which are realistic and which are imagined? Once they are familiar with their chosen page, ask pupils to imagine they have the camera shown in the story and that they are travelling around their chosen location. Use guided fantasy/role-play/discussion to help pupils think about what that place is like. If they zoom in to one of the homes what can they see? Challenge them to make a floor plan or a pictorial representation of what the home looks like. In making and discussing their plans, pupils will use geographical vocabulary, including directional and descriptive language.

Digital underwater worlds

Flotsam acts as a great stimulus for pupils to imagine and create their own fantastical underwater worlds. Ask them to imagine they are taking a journey through the ocean with the camera. What can they see/hear/smell? What objects and colours can they see? What is happening in the ocean? Pupils should share their journey with a talk partner.

Using play dough, clay or plasticine, pupils make a 3D model of what they imagine the ocean to be like. When complete, take digital photographs of their models. These could be used either in a PowerPoint presentation to create a digital story or inserted into Windows Movie Maker to make a film. In this way the movement of the film simulates a sense of movement through the water. Once the digital story has been created and shared, ask pupils to compare and contrast their imaginary worlds. This creates exciting opportunities for pupils to engage in oral and written descriptions of imaginary places and the possibility of writing new stories.

Hear that place

This activity requires a set of musical instruments and multiple copies of pages from the book. Divide the class into small groups and assign each group one page of the book. Pupils imagine they are fish moving around that location. They should think about the different objects and movements in that location, and use the instruments to create sounds to represent the place.

Creating a sound map to show the way around the place will help groups of pupils to organise a performance to the class, perhaps with one of the group acting as the conductor. In composing and sharing their music, pupils will be encouraged to think about the characteristics of their particular location.

Living graphs

Share *Flotsam* and write or draw the order of places presented in the story. Ask pupils to think about how they would feel if they were in each of the places, exploring the language of emotions and range of feelings places provoke. Use a living graph to record this work. Along the horizontal axis, pupils draw the places visited and along the vertical axis they draw a range of feelings from sad to happy. Pupils plot their feelings about each place, creating a line graph which they then annotate and compare with others.

27

Belonging
Jeannie Baker, Walker Books (2004)

This book has an urban Australian setting

Geographical enquiry and skills

- enquiry – asking and answering questions
- visual literacy – using pictures to identify change
- geographical imagination – imagining future changes

Geographical knowledge and understanding

- features of urban environments/settlements
- environmental changes
- sustainable transport
- local communities
- the impact of individual and community actions
- the importance of green spaces in urban environments
- 'greening' urban environments
- urban wildlife habitats

To access extra resources from the Everyday Guides web page, see page 2.

This award-winning picture book shows the changing view through the window of a house over a period of 24 years. Whereas the author's previous book, *Window*, shows the gradual encroachment of urban developments in an initially rural area, *Belonging* depicts the reverse, from an almost entirely built-up environment, through gradual greening, until the area is verdantly transformed. The changes are depicted through beautiful collages. Primary pupils of all ages are likely to enjoy this book. The pictures are full of intriguing details that encourage careful scrutiny. The key messages are that urban environments can be made greener to provide suitable habitats for plants and wildlife and that individuals can make a difference through seemingly small initiatives.

Sharing the book

Start by showing the front cover and ask what pupils can see. Draw their attention to the oblique bird's-eye view and list the features they name. Where do they think the book is set? If necessary, introduce the word 'urban'. Compare the environment depicted in the book with an urban environment pupils know (such as the local area) and identify common features. As you read the book, encourage pupils to note the changes and the passage of time. Show the back cover – another bird's-eye view but this time of a house and surrounding area. Again ask what pupils can see and create a second list of the features. Consider the differences between the two lists. Note that the back cover also depicts an urban area, but one that has been transformed. Introduce appropriate vocabulary to discuss these changes (e.g. sustainable development, environmental improvements and greening).

Ask pupils which environment they would rather live in and why. They could record their thoughts on speech bubble-shaped sticky notes. Finally, open up the cover to reveal that the front and back show two adjacent areas, sharing roads and buildings. This is likely to provoke gasps of surprise and elicit further discussion.

Teaching activities

Looking through our window

Ask pupils to look through the classroom window and to consider what they see. What features enhance the view? What opportunities for greening can they see? How would they like it to change? How do they imagine the view might look in the future – in two years, five years, ten years, next century?

Use pupil responses as the stimulus for a number of activities focusing on future changes. You could provide photographs showing the current view and ask pupils to draw how they think it will look in the future; you or they could choose the timescale. A sheet with an appropriately shaped window frame will help pupils to work at the right scale.

Alternatively, you could ask them to show how the view could change in 24 years (the period of time in *Belonging*) if local people tried to make the area greener and more sustainable. Pupils could annotate the current view photograph or draw their vision for the future.

Invite pupils to undertake similar activities focusing on the view from their bedroom window. This will be enhanced if they can use digital cameras to take a photograph.

Environmental changes

Ask pupils to study the changes shown in *Belonging* and work in pairs to record them on sticky notes (one change per note) then sort them into different categories. Pupils can generate their own categories or work with some you suggest. Possibilities include changes: in gardens; in land use; buildings and open space; in transport; for plants and wildlife; in the activities people are doing; that children could initiate; after different periods of time (e.g. 6 years/12 years/18 years/24 years).

Consider all the changes noted, then invite pupils to evaluate these from different perspectives such as: easiest to achieve; would most improve life for children; are most costly; need collective action; are within the power of individuals; have the most impact for wildlife; are most desirable. Ask pupils to sequence the sticky notes on a line, from the easiest to achieve to the most difficult to achieve. Ask different groups to explore different changes and then to consider and comment on each group's thoughts in turn.

Greening our school grounds/local area

Undertake a class investigation into the possibilities for greening the school grounds or the local area. Ideally, this should be an authentic learning activity – i.e. one which involves a real purpose, audience and outcome – and should provide plenty of opportunities for all elements of an enquiry. It should involve asking questions about what could be improved; working together to plan and conduct the enquiry; choosing skills, resources and techniques to investigate the feasibility and desirability of potential improvements; reflecting on the outcomes of the investigation; communicating the conclusions to relevant stakeholders; and evaluating the whole enquiry process and what has been learnt and achieved.

The eco-schools website offers resources for practical projects to improve biodiversity in the school grounds, and the Royal Horticultural Society website offers advice on urban greening and school gardening (see Everyday Guides web page for links).

The Other Side of Truth
Beverley Naidoo, Puffin (2000)

This book is set in Lagos, Nigeria, and London, England

Geographical enquiry and skills

- enquiry – asking and answering questions
- map making
- map reading
- route planning
- using secondary sources to research distant localities

Geographical knowledge and understanding

- location of places in *The Other Side of Truth*
- what it means to be a refugee and seek asylum
- reasons for migration
- the impact of political tyranny
- citizenship and national boundaries

Twelve year-old Sade and her ten year-old brother Femi witness political unrest during which their mother is shot dead in Lagos, Nigeria. The bullet was meant for their father – a journalist critical of the Nigerian government. For their safety, Sade and Femi are smuggled out of Nigeria and find themselves abandoned in London. Immigration officers take the children into care, finding foster homes and schools for them. The book describes the process of being admitted to England as a refugee for the children, and eventually, their father. This award-wining novel explores the consequences of political dissent against tyranny. It is likely to touch the hearts and minds of all who read it.

Sharing the book

Before reading the book, ask pupils why and how people move between countries. Discuss their ideas and record their initial understandings about migration, refugees and asylum seekers. Use questions to ensure that they consider the concept of forced movement. On a piece of paper with 'home' written in the centre, pupils should mind-map key words and ideas about what home means to them and to other children around the world. This will enable pupils to put the story in context.

To access extra resources from the Everyday Guides web page, see page 2.

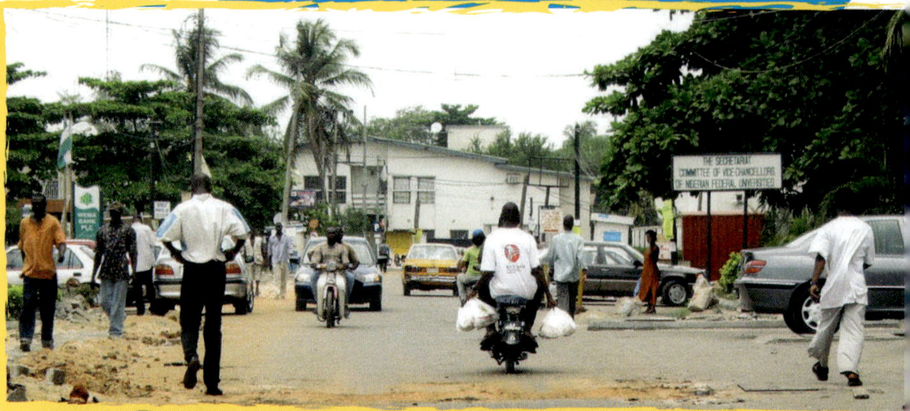

Teaching activities

Working wall

As you read *The Other Side of Truth*, create a working wall to display pupils' reflections, questions and new understandings. This can be made simply by backing a display board with plain paper, and could include the following:

- A map that charts the routes that Femi and Sade take as the plot develops. Use atlases, globes and the internet to find out about the places mentioned. Encourage pupils to reflect on the emotions Sade and Femi experience in the different places and annotate the map with emoticons to reflect these.
- A chart with two categories: plot and place. Following each chapter, ask pupils to summarise the plot and list information they have found out about place(s) in that chapter. In plenary sessions, ask them to find connections between plot and place. How is the plot affected by where the story is taking place? How are characters reactions affected by the situation(s)/place(s) they find themselves in?
- In Chapter 3 Sade and Femi are forced to pack a small rucksack to take to London. Ask pupils to put themselves in the children's place: what would they pack for the journey?

Exploring migration patterns

Ask pupils to find out where their parents, aunts, uncles and grandparents were born and where they live now. Each pupil then annotates an individual map showing all these locations. This is likely to provoke discussions about different map scales – some pupils may need world maps, while others require only a local street map.

Invite pupils to identify some relatives and ask them why they moved from their childhood home. As a class, record all the different reasons people move – to study, for work, for better opportunities, to escape religious or political persecution, because of personal relationships, etc. Consider how these reasons can be sorted into 'push' and 'pull' factors, i.e. push: negative factors which encourage people to leave a place, and pull: positive factors which attract them to another place. Pupils should also say where they would like to live when they are adults, and why. You can use the activity sheet 'Exploring why people move' available from the Everyday Guides web page.

The complex issues involved in decisions to migrate/forced migration could be explored in circle time or through a Philosophy for Children (P4C) enquiry.

Geographical imagery

The author, Beverly Naidoo, uses many striking geographical images and metaphors which could be used to spark discussion/philosophy sessions or act as a stimulus for creative arts or writing. To extend the activity, use phrases from *The Other Side of Truth* as a basis for questionning. Ask pupils to consider how the images in the novel impact on their understanding and appreciation of the world.

'At that moment she and Femi were like two parcels with no address. They could end up anywhere.'

- How would this feel?
- What action can children take if they are lost or afraid?

'A map would have shown a magnificent giant spider's web, with dozens of strands drawing in toward Family House.'

- What places do pupils know that are like a spider's web?
- Invite pupils to create art work, a dance, a play or an installation on the theme of their school or other significant place, such as a religious building, as the hub of a web of connections and activity.

'For a little while they stared without speaking at this world inside a world.'

- Discuss what this quote might mean and what Femi and Sade were seeing that was different to their usual experiences. Ask if anyone in the class has had an experience like this. Why does this feeling sometimes come about with new places or changes?

31

In the Bush: Our holiday at Wombat Flat

Roland Harvey, Allen and Unwin (2005)

This book is set in the bush in the Australian Alps

Geographical enquiry and skills

- enquiry – asking and answering questions
- visual literacy – using pictures to stimulate interest in the landscapes of the Australian outback
- map work – using and making maps
- using secondary sources

Geographical knowledge and understanding

- the location of significant places in Australia
- the varied landscape, climate and animals of the Australian Alps
- leisure activities in the Australian outback
- leisure activities in the local area and beyond

Reference

Potter, C. and Scoffham, S. (2006) 'Emotional maps', *Primary Geographer*, 60, pp. 20–1.

To access extra resources from the Everyday Guides web page, see page 2.

This picture book for older primary children follows the adventures of a family on a camping holiday in the Australian outback. Each double-page spread shows a bird's-eye view of a different aspect of the bush landscape and is swarming with numerous tiny figures engaged in multitudinous activities. The family members take turns to provide chatty commentary on the holiday as it unfolds. Children will love the humour in the drawings, and will enjoy spotting the various misadventures described by the family members. *In the Bush* includes a variety of maps, including a sketch map of Wombat Flat and a simple star map.

Enjoy the book

In the Bush is best read by individuals or in pairs/small groups, as much of the fun is in studying the details in the comic illustrations and in trying to relate the incidents briefly described in the text to the pictures. Pupils can try to find the family members among the hordes of holiday makers and locate the incidents described in the brief commentary in the illustration.

Teaching activities

Investigating the Australian Alps

Challenge pupils to investigate the Australian Alps using the internet, holiday brochures and travel guides. What attracts holiday makers to the Australian Alps? What would it be like to live there? Invite pupils to choose how to present their findings – as posters, digital presentations, travel itineraries, or even their own imagined travel diary.

Mapping significant incidents

One of the most engaging features of *In the Bush* is the sketch map of Wombat Flat and the surrounding area, annotated with notes about incidents shown in the book. Replicate this idea by producing a map of the school grounds or local area for pupils to annotate with their memories of significant events. If possible, provide a large-scale base map or ask pupils to make a sketch map. Invite them to note their memories on small sticky notes and place these on the map in the correct location. They are likely to recall events of emotional significance. The article by Potter and Scoffham (2006) provides further ideas on emotional mapping.

Investigating tourism

In the Bush could act as a stimulus for a wide range of open-ended tasks relating to the geographical aspects of camping/outdoor activities and tourism more generally. These include:

- Designing a website/holiday brochure/poster for Wombat Flat.
- Designing an ideal campsite, incorporating all the features the pupils would like.
- Writing a diary or blog of a stay at Wombat Flat, possibly as one of the ancillary characters in the story.
- Designing postcards to be sold in a shop near Wombat Flat.
- Creating a picture map of the Wombat Flat campsite.
- Keeping a journal about their holidays in the style of the book.
- Investigating local campsites – What facilities do they have? Who uses them? Where have visitors travelled from? Why is the site located where it is?
- Investigating pupils' views on different types of holidays, exploring the range of factors which influence holiday choices.
- Considering the environmental impact of tourism and how it can be made more sustainable.

© Andrea Schaffer (Creative Commons licence)

Kensuke's Kingdom
Michael Morpurgo, Egmont UK Ltd (2005)

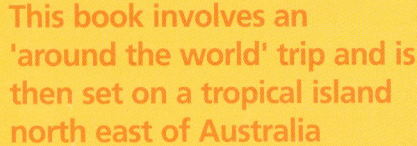

This book involves an 'around the world' trip and is then set on a tropical island north east of Australia

Geographical enquiry and skills

- enquiry – asking and answering questions
- atlas work – using atlas maps to follow and plan routes
- map work – using and making maps
- using secondary sources to find out about other countries/ports of call

Geographical knowledge and understanding

- world locational knowledge – continents, countries, oceans and seas
- the characteristics of specific named places (e.g. ports of call)
- needs and wants of different people
- sustainable lifestyles
- how people use available resources to meet their needs
- intercultural understanding

To access extra resources from the Everyday Guides web page, see page 2.

© theswedish/stock.xchng

This short novel for older primary children tells the story of what happens when 11-year-old Michael is shipwrecked on a sea voyage. Finding himself washed up on a deserted Pacific island with nothing to eat or drink, Michael curls up to die. When he wakes, however, someone has left food and water beside him…

The short chapters offer many opportunities for geographical, literacy and cross-curricular work. Chapters 1 and 2 set the scene and describe life aboard the *Peggy Sue*, while Chapter 3 comprises extracts from the ship's log. The shipwreck occurs in Chapter 4, and later chapters describe subsequent events on the island. The book includes a map of the island on which Michael finds himself stranded.

Kensuke's Kingdom covers important themes including survival in hostile environments; building relationships; communicating without common language or culture; and the importance of respect for others' choices and lifestyles

Sharing the book

This is a great novel to read aloud. The key moments of decision, tension or conflict can be explored through movement, drama or discussion. For example, pupils can role play the moment Michael finds himself alone on the beach, when Michael and Kensuke first meet, or when the gibbon hunters approach the island.

Teaching activities

Mapping the voyage

While he is travelling one of Michael's tasks is to keep the ship's log up to date. As you read, use a globe and world map to track the ship's route. Create a display using a world map to record the journey. Ask small groups of pupils to research the ports of call using the internet, atlases, information books and holiday brochures. The groups can share their findings by writing letters or postcards to Michael's best friend Eddie or his Gran. Alternatively, they could create posters designed to promote the cities Michael visits to other tourists. Display these alongside the world map.

Pupils could also plan their own round-the-world trip. Offer a choice of challenges – to design a route incorporating one country in every continent, to travel only by rail and sea, to use as many different forms of transport as possible – or make the task entirely open-ended. Many contemporary round-the-world sailors write blogs, and following the progress of a real voyage in real time would enrich this work.

Mapping/modelling the island

As the story unfolds, we learn more about the island and its features. Use the descriptions of Michael's explorations as the basis for making maps or models of the island with pupils, adding more details as they are revealed. Older pupils could create a fabric play mat, papier-mâché model or pop-up picture of an island for younger children to use in imaginative play.

Wants and needs

Working in a large space, ask pupils to imagine themselves as Michael curled up on the beach. They then act out waking to find that he and his dog have survived. Invite them to explore through mime or role play their first thoughts and actions and then to share these orally. What does Michael need to survive? Continue this guided fantasy, asking pupils to act out exploring the island – seeking but failing to find fresh water and food. How does this make them feel?

Consider what humans need to survive further by completing the wants and needs card sorting activity (see Everyday Guides web page). This is likely to provoke discussions about not only physiological needs for food, water and shelter, but also psychological needs such as for feeling safe, love and companionship.

Later in *Kensuke's Kingdom*, we learn how Kensuke has survived on the island. Invite pupils to compare the ways in which they and Kensuke meet their basic needs, recording this as a chart or diagram. Kensuke's water, food, means of transport, etc., are derived directly from his environment; although it is not so immediately apparent, help pupils to understand that their needs are also met by the resources of the environment. Pupils should also consider how Kensuke has met his psychological and social needs during his long years of isolation.

Intercultural understanding

Ask pupils to reflect on how, despite having no common language or shared culture, Michael and Kensuke build a relationship. What is the initial cause of suspicion and conflict in their relationship? How does this come to be gradually replaced by a deep respect and love for one another? Create a timeline of the key events, and note the strategies Kensuke and Michael use to try to communicate with and understand each other.

© jdnx (Creative Commons licence)

Useful resources

Arizpe, E. and Styles, M. (2003) *Children Reading Pictures: Interpreting visual texts*. London: RoutledgeFalmer.

Ballin, B. (2012) 'Tell it again: breathing life into places', *Primary Geography*, 78, p. 11.

Bower, J. (2005) *Practical Creativity at Key Stages 1 and 2*. New York NY: RoutledgeFalmer.

Boyce, L. (ed) (1999) *A Different Story: Literacy to open up the world at key stage 2*. Birmingham: Teachers in Development Education.

Bromley, H. (2007) *50 Exciting Ideas for Story Boxes*. Birmingham: Lawrence Educational Publications.

Catling, S. and Willy, T. (2009) *Teaching Primary Geography*. Exeter: Learning Matters.

Cremin, T. (2009) *Teaching English Creatively*. Abingdon: Routledge.

Daniel, A.K. (2011) *Storytelling Across the Primary Curriculum*. Abingdon: Routledge.

Dolan, A. (2013) 'Geography and stories' in Scoffham, S. (ed) *Teaching Geography Creatively*. London: Routledge, pp. 31–46.

Duncan, D. (2008) *Teaching Children's Literature: Making stories work in the classroom*. London: Routledge.

Evans, J. (2009) *Talking Beyond the Page: Reading and responding to picturebooks*. New York NY: Routledge.

Lewis, L. (2010) 'Geography and language development' in Scoffham, S. (ed) *Primary Geography Handbook*. Sheffield: Geographical Association, pp. 148–63.

Salisbury, M. and Styles, M. (2012) *Children's Picturebooks: The art of visual storytelling*. London: Laurence King Publishing.

Scoffham, S. (ed) (2010) *Primary Geography Handbook*. Sheffield: Geographical Association.

Scoffham, S. (ed) (2012) *Teaching Geography Creatively*. London: Routledge.

Short, K. (2009) 'Critically reading the word and the world: building intercultural understanding through literature', *Bookbird: A Journal of International Children's Literature*, 47, 2, pp. 1–10. Available online at http://wowlit.org/Documents/LangandCultureKitDocs/22CriticallyReadingtheWorld.pdf (last accessed 6 August 2012).

Short, K. (2012) 'Engaging pupils in dialogue', *Primary Geography*, 78, pp. 6–7.

Teachers in Development Education (TIDE~) (2002) *Start with a Story: Supporting young children's exploration of issues*. Birmingham: Teachers in Development Education.

Wray, D. (2006) *Teaching Literacy across the Primary Curriculum*. Exeter: Learning Matters.

Relevant materials on the GA website

Teaching ideas for maps and stories ages 4–11: www.geography.org.uk/projects/primaryhandbook/mapsandstories

Foundation stage use of the fictional text *The Journey*: www.geography.org.uk/projects/younggeographers/resources/austrey

KS1 use of poems and stories to introduce environmental issues: www.geography.org.uk/projects/younggeographers/resources/joylane

KS1 using traditional tales to develop fieldwork and film media: www.geography.org.uk/projects/younggeographers/resources/southborough

www.geography.org.uk/eyprimary/geographyliteracy/bookreviews/#top

Other useful links

www.booktrust.org.uk/books-and-reading

www.booktrust.org.uk/professionals/teacher/everybody-writes-project

www.ukla.org/resources/category/fiction

www.literacytrust.org.uk/guide

www.tidec.org/primary-early-years

http://creativeeducator.tech4learning.com/v05/articles/Digital_Storytelling_Across_the_Curriculum

www.storyarts.org/lessonplans/acrosscurriculum/index.html

http://editlib.org/p/22131

www.globaldimension.org.uk/resources